Praise for *Out of the Trenches*

As a long-time educator, I know what it feels like to be in the trenches. In this book, Dana Goodier explores not just how we find ourselves in the trenches, but provides her roadmap for the journey to success. Resiliency is a key focus of this excellent book. I am confident that educators in all stages of their careers will resonate with the humanity of this story...an important lesson on self-reflection and growth.

Martin Silverman
Principal, Author, Presenter, San Antonio, Texas

Out of the Trenches destigmatizes the natural process of growth everyone encounters when doing something new and challenging. Every reader will find something to relate to in Dana's personal stories and inclusion of stories from her *Out of the Trenches* podcast. This book is reassuring and lets readers know that they are not alone and to keep going!

Heather Lyon
Educator, Author of *Engagement is Not a Unicorn (It's a Narwhal)* & *The BIG Book of Engagement Strategies*

Overcome challenges and learn strategies to invest in yourself, students, teachers, and families. *Out of the Trenches: Stories of Resilient Educators* can help you develop and hone your educational skills, pointing you and those you work with on a path to make a difference for others. This book is a must-read for anyone in education. Every person in a school can learn strategies to get out of the trenches!

Evan Robb
Author, Speaker Principal

Out of the Trenches is a melange of marvelous stories based on Dana's many outreaches to educators through her podcast, She has highlighted those educators and their practices to bring a comprehensive perspective of common sense and careful planning to those who are having a positive effect on their students, their schools, and their communities. Out of the Trenches is written in praise of effective, common sense education,

Joseph Pizzo
Teacher, Adjunct Professor, Poet, Podcaster

Resiliency is a topic that is needed in our field of service. Dana does an excellent job of capturing the essence of how we can all be resilient, all while being inspired by the stories of others. This book was definitely just what my heart needed in this season of life.

Todd Nesloney
Director of Culture & Strategic Leadership at TEPSA

Dana nails her description of being in the trenches. But we don't want to stay there! Read Dana's journey and get her advice about how she and others learned from the good and bad of others.

James Divine
Educator, Motivational Speaker

Out of the Trenches: Stories of Resilient Educators by Dana Goodier is a book to help educators know we are not alone. The educator trench stories are powerful examples of reflection, resilience, persistence, and growth. An inspiring read to support us all on our unique journeys as educators. These relatable stories are for all educators. As we continue this work to support student growth, *Out of the Trenches* helps us to not forget to focus on ourselves too. We deserve it and can learn from one another.

Stephanie Rothstein
Education Innovation Leader, Speaker, Writer

Out of the Trenches captures the essence of an educator in a way that not many books can. The way that Dana is able to weave together motivation, with practical tools and resources to increase resiliency of any educator is truly remarkable. Dana uses personal stories, and the stories of other educators to highlight real-life resiliency that will inspire and motivate any educator feeling burned out or who may be in need of a little extra reminder of their own personal why! The strategies provided are easy to implement and will have a major impact on your own resiliency as an educator! This one is a must-read for any educator looking to further connect with themselves regardless of where they are on their professional journey!

Lindsay Titus
Assistant Principal, Coach,
Speaker with Define YOUniversity

Dana's thoughtful words push past the generic "What's your WHY?" in education and redefines how to refuel goals to get out of the trenches and back to a healthy mindset with purpose. The contribution and resilient examples of others' journeys in this narrative shows there is no limit to the power of perseverance and grit. The common thread woven throughout the chapters is that those challenging times in the trenches can lead to great aptitude for seeing the positives despite the circumstances.

Jillian Dubois
Educator, Author, Illustrator

Dr. Goodier's book takes us deep into the trenches of leaders and educators who forged their philosophies and careers around the frontline work that makes for the most compelling stories. She has collected an incredible array of representation to speak to leaders, teachers, and families everywhere about the wonders and hardships of serving in the education profession. For anyone who has ever needed an authentic, exciting story to motivate their work and life, this is the one for you.

Matthew J. Bowerman
School Administrator, Author, Speaker, Artist

Dana Goodier's *Out of the Trenches: Stories of Resilient Educators* is a timely reminder to educators who have been battered by the events of the last two plus years. Her trench stories are uplifting and shared with humility and grace. Whether you are a seasoned veteran, an aspiring leader, or a new to the ranks educator, you will find something for you within the stories and strategies shared in these pages. You can devour the stories all in one go, or take it an anecdote/strategy at a time, let it percolate, digest it and let it lift you from your current trench. These stories are worth revisiting time and again as you need!

Terence Tong, M. Ed.
International Educator, Aspiring Leader

In *Out of the Trenches*, Dana Goodier provides story after story of educators who got knocked down and picked themselves back up. It's not IF you will be knocked down in your career, but rather, WHEN it will happen and HOW you will respond. Read this book to grow your Resilience.

Danny Bauer
Chief Ruckus Maker

Out of the Trenches
Stories of Resilient Educators

Dana Goodier, EdD

Out of the Trenches: Stories of Resilient Educators

Copyright © by Dana Goodier
First Edition 2022

All rights reserved.

No part of this publication may be reproduced in any form, or by any means, electronic or mechanical, including photocopying, recording, or any information browsing, storage or retrieval system, without permission in writing from the publisher.

Road to Awesome, LLC.

I dedicate my first book to my family.
I would like to thank my husband, Jesse Soklin, and my three kids for their support during each podcast pre-chat meeting and recordings I have had along with meetings with my publisher that sometimes take place during the evenings and weekends.

Table of Contents

Introduction..1

Chapter 1 – Staring Down the Trench................................5

Chapter 2 – A Helping Hand Out of the Trench................17

Chapter 3 – Climbing out of the Trench........................... 29

Chapter 4 – Finding What Makes Your Passion Grow.........39

Chapter 5 – Keeping Yourself Out of the Trenches............ 51

Chapter 6 – Thriving in the Trenches................................ 63

Conclusion.. 69

Recommendations to Improve Your Practice.....................73

Acknowledgements..77

References...79

About the Author.. 85

Work With Dana... 87

Introduction

Most people have heard the phrase *in the trenches* at some point in their lives. My definition of in the trenches is being in a difficult situation where you feel stuck for a time but manage to crawl out and learn resiliency from the experience. Resilience can be defined as the ability to persevere. But according to García & Miralles, who wrote *Ikigai: The Japanese Secret to a Long and Healthy Life,* resilience is also an outlook we gain by staying focused on the most important things in life, so as to not get carried away with negative thoughts and emotions. The way we face our most difficult challenges in life makes a huge difference in the quality of our lives. I have seen it play out many times in my own home.

Having many trench stories of my own and wanted a platform to highlight the struggles other educators may have been through and why they persevered. The idea to start my own podcast came after I started listening to a few educational leadership podcasts in 2017. But I did not have the time to actually work on this idea until I finished my EdD in March 2020. After a conversation with a respected podcaster about how to get started, I decided to go ahead and launch my podcast, *Out of the Trenches*, in May of 2020. I wasn't sure I would have enough to offer or could live up to the dynamic possessed by the podcast hosts I had listened to. Nevertheless, I got into the flow of interviewing guests, and after a few months, I had interviewed several guests that had gone through trenches similar to mine.

You'll read stories of resilience from educators who were guests on my podcast as well as excerpts of my own story and how we navigated the twists and turns of our trenches in order to thrive in our careers. You will have the chance to think about your own experiences and when you may have found yourself in a trench. It is my hope that you will learn how to define or redefine your purpose within your career and discover ways to navigate challenges that may change your why.

If a job or otherwise sticky situation has you looking for a way out, the stories in this book will empower you to crawl, climb, walk or run out of that trench. I will outline the steps to provide you with tools to come out of your own trench and stay out.

You don't have to spend forever in your trenches. Take it from me, when you have been through multiple trenches, you learn to pick yourself up and move forward. Reading this book will give you insight into how you can manage to get out of a difficult situation and thrive in your career in education.

This book isn't meant as a rah-rah to say that everything is great in education. We all know that educators have one of the hardest jobs in the world. However, those who truly are in it to make a difference tend to stick with it, though it may take multiple iterations and roles in education to find where they can truly make that difference.

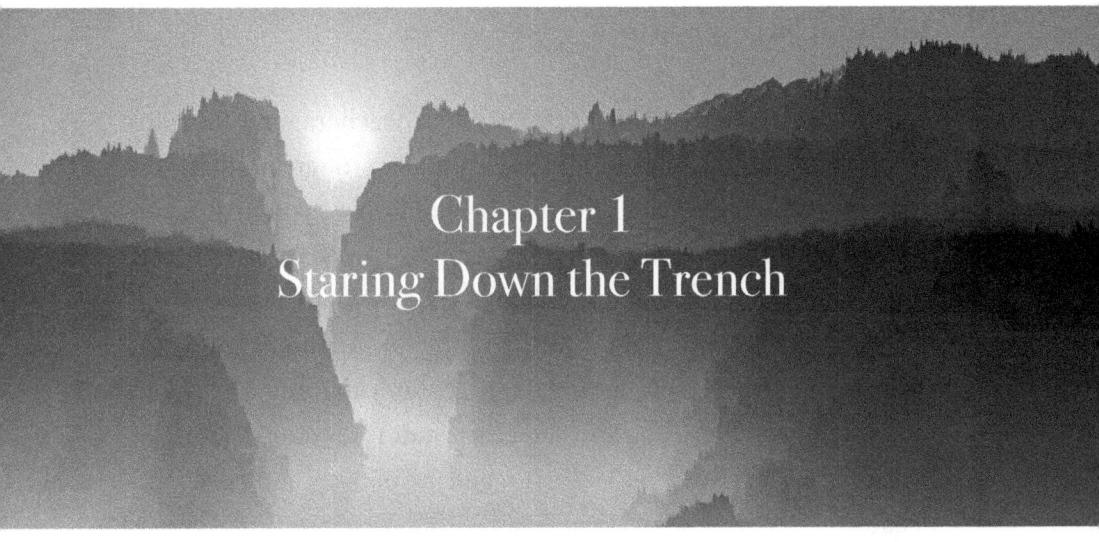

Chapter 1
Staring Down the Trench

The beginning of my teaching career trench story involved working with expert, cooperating teachers during my student teaching. Being new to the profession, I wasn't familiar with the little bits of knowledge teachers gain over time about things such as holding your bladder for several hours and dressing like a professional teacher (by late 1990s standards). Those things, at the time, seemed to be all the cooperative teachers wanted me to do, i.e., not to excuse myself if I desperately needed to use the restroom during class even when they were in the room. The only feedback I remember getting was not about my instruction but about my attire. "Wear more skirts and blouses," the high school cooperating teacher encouraged, and gave me two long peasant skirts as a send-off gift at the end of the semester. This picky treatment about whether I dressed like teachers a good 25 years older than me made me feel incapable of truly being able to spread my wings and fly with my student teaching classroom. The two cooperating teachers I had (one for each subject in which I was being certified) were so protective of their classrooms that they barely left them over to me to grow and learn.

Luckily, things have changed for student teachers, and they are given many more weeks to take over the classroom and teach on their own. Looking back, I probably should have reached out to the university student–teacher coordinator at several intervals during that semester and asked her to speak with the cooperating teachers about how little I was getting to teach on my own. Instead, I sat back, did as I thought I was supposed to do and quietly remained a shadow in the classroom I was supposed to be learning to teach in, an observer and a follower rather than a leader.

After those not-so-great days of student teaching, it would be over two years until I taught again at the secondary level. I spent those two years pursuing my PhD in the field of linguistics in Québec, Canada, my first attempt. I was also teaching adult continuing education at the university. Roughly two months into my first classroom experience at the secondary level, I realized just how grossly unprepared I was as a result of my student teaching experience.

Most people can attest that they often took everything personally when they received constructive criticism. They fully thought they were the expert as a new teacher. Often, as a first-year teacher, you get thrown in headfirst. You use your instincts (sometimes those are survival instincts). You may have a mentor teacher or supportive colleagues but are afraid to ask them about things you're not sure of for fear of what they may think of you.

As a high school electives teacher, I often taught freshmen. Most high school teachers would agree that this is a difficult transition year. In 2002, I went from teaching college students and adults to teaching 9th-12th graders. Like many new teachers, I had classroom management issues. I was taught during my teacher prep program to enforce the rules. It wasn't until many years later that I brought students on board to help create a class code of conduct, allowing them to take ownership of their behavior in the classroom. If you had visited my classroom in the early 2000s, you would have cringed watching me read a four- or five-page list of rules and expectations, along with the syllabus, on the first day of school! Let's just say the long list of "do-nots" didn't sit well with some students. They tested the boundaries. They learned how to get a reaction out of me, and I took things personally. I did not get much support that first year and did not return to that school for a second year. This was, in part, due to the enrollment in French classes going down when the U.S. invaded Iraq in the Spring of 2003 and France didn't support the invasion (remember Freedom Fries?). I had to find my way to another environment and another school where I could fulfill my purpose in my career. The journey to finding a place where I was able to thrive and make a difference teaching French took another two years.

Recognizing signs of burnout and dissatisfaction with your daily work routine could be a clue that you are in a trench. If you think to yourself that some days you don't care about the money you'd lose if you broke your contract, you just want to get out of the job you're currently in, then you're burned out. When you come home drained every day because you are devoting your all to your job without taking any time for mental health breaks, you're burned out. When you consider leaving the profession and never looking back, even if you don't have a backup plan, you're burned out. When you're able to identify signs of burnout, you can move forward and decide what you want to do about it.

Amber Harper was on a roller coaster of burnout. Amber loved teaching and she loved her students. She even went through periods where she also got along wonderfully with her colleagues and teaching team. Other times, she didn't. When she was struggling with teaching and dealing with teacher burnout, she would try to talk about it, but those conversations always ended up as a venting session. When she felt this way, she was told to go for a walk, take a bubble bath, take some deep breaths, or go buy herself something nice. But what she was frustrated by was that she *did* practice self-care. She exercised every day, ate healthy foods, and drank plenty of water. She did all these things to help herself be a healthy, happy teacher. When she was truly challenged she wanted to do something about it rather than be looked at as a negative teacher, but she didn't know how to voice what was challenging her. It seemed to her, during this whole roller coaster ride, that there was something wrong with her, that this couldn't be normal.

A lot of times teachers don't have a support system and they're afraid to reach out to their colleagues. Sometimes, they feel less than competent, as if there's something wrong with them. Amber left the classroom to have more balance in her life and created Burned-In Teacher, burned-out teacher coaching. It's what she always needed when she was in the trenches, and she wanted to activate a teacher's self-empowerment. She wanted teachers to go from feeling like victims of circumstance to taking chances and allow them to work through their burnout. Amber's way to beat burnout is growing through the burnout. She has learned that burnout is truly an opportunity; it's a call for change in action.

Amber went back to teaching at the kindergarten level but continues to coach burned out teachers as well. She is also a podcaster and speaker. Using the tools she developed through her website, speaking, and consulting, you can evaluate your level of burnout and become a burned-IN educator.

Scan for the full episode.

Sometimes, educators can get so deep in the trench that they turn to unhealthy habits. They may feel it's the only way to deal with the level of stress they feel on a daily basis.

Rick Jetter, PhD, is the Assistant Head of Schools at the Western New York Maritime Charter School and the Co-Founder of Pushing Boundaries Consulting. He is also an educator, author, speaker, and national education consultant. He felt that getting out of the trench was like pulling himself out of hell, a situation he goes into detail about in his book *Escaping the School Leader's Dunk Tank: How to Prevail When Others Want to See You Drown*. Rick was a superintendent working in a high-functioning school district where there were some Board of Education revenge initiatives. This mentality started trickling into the environment. As superintendent, he felt like all he was doing was protecting the district from legal issues. He started drinking heavily, became an alcoholic and took prescription medications during this difficult time in his life. It became his mechanism to cope with the chaos. He feels as if he wrote his own ticket to hell but got himself out by seeking refuge in rehab. Rick calls his alcoholism a self-inflicted nightmare. Eventually, he found joy in his position as an Assistant Head of Schools. Looking back, Rick sees that part of his life as a trench he pulled himself out of but learned a great deal from in the process.

Rick reminds us to use our driving force and find our purpose, even if it goes down a winding path. He thinks a lot of educators hold back when telling their story. He advises writers to shake it up, and talk about the things people don't want to talk about. He thinks educators need to share their recoveries, as he has done in his e-book *Recovery Mode: Educators Emerging from Unexpected and Rapid Change*.

Scan for the full episode.

If your level of stress gets to the point of anxiety and it's affecting your work, there are ways to manage this. One of these ways is through mindfulness practices. These practices have been around for a long time but have really come to the forefront in society since 2020. There are many apps and programs that work with you to learn which mindfulness strategies will work best for your situation.

Sherianna Boyle, author of the Emotional Detox book series and founder of Emotional Detox Coaching® found herself in the trenches early in her career as a school psychologist. She was getting ready to go on maternity leave and get her position ready for a long-term substitute. This is when she really became aware of feeling anxiety. Once she had her daughter, Sherianna's anxiety did not abate, leaving her feeling like she was in a trench again. After analyzing her situation, she realized the anxiety began well before the birth of her baby. She spoke to her doctor and was prescribed an antidepressant. That one didn't work, so they tried another and another. Sherianna tried five antidepressants in one year as a new mom. None of them worked, and all of that medication was starting to affect her liver. She decided she didn't want to be dealing with these types of health problems so early in her life and started researching mindfulness approaches to curb her anxiety. This research gave her the idea to write the first of many books on using mindfulness practices to help with anxiety, among other things. Sherianna pulled herself out of this trench mindfully.

Scan for the full episode.

She developed her Emotional Detox® system to help people connect with and process their emotions. Many people try to push their emotions to the back of their mind with the hope that they will just go away. Emotional Detox® is based on the idea that all emotions are good, so long as you process them. When we process our emotions we gain wisdom and insight. Emotions can be nourishing to your body and mind.

I have gained a great deal of insight into dealing with conflicts by practicing mindfulness. I try to be proactive, rather than reactive. I won't say that's always how I respond, depending on the seriousness of the situation. We all have our own threshold of tolerance for the situations life hands us.

Although she was very shy all throughout childhood and into high school, Orly Fortune Wahba had known since she was four years old that she wanted to do something to change the world. Her shyness made the transition from grade school to secondary school difficult. Many of her friends moved on to other social groups, without Orly. Not only did she feel alone from the loss of her friends, but then her family lost everything in a fire that burned down their home. Her parents didn't know how they would put food on the table, and the family was unable to live together for years.

Orly had descended into a deep depression by the time she was in high school. She was unable to pull herself out of this place of sadness, anger and loneliness. She was out of school for months due to her depression, yet no one called or visited. She wondered, if she was not there tomorrow, would she be missed. She felt the answer was no. She felt like a shell of a person who no longer wanted to live. She was forced to go back to school, but she just didn't care about anything anymore.

One day, she was in the bathroom getting ready for school, and she really looked at herself in the mirror. She did not recognize herself; she could no longer see that four-year-old Orly. And that scared her more than anything. At that moment, she made a promise to herself to be there for people the way she wished somebody would have been there for her, to see people the way she wished someone would have seen her. That promise guided her to her seven years of teaching, to start her organization about kindness, and it wakes her up everyday. After that, Orly was able to, eventually, see herself for who she really was and find her voice.

Orly Fortune Wahba is the founder of the global non-profit Life Vest Inside, a kindness expert, educator, and entrepreneur who inspires people to act. Her organization's mission is to inspire, empower and educate people of all backgrounds to lead a life of kindness. The organization grew from the recognition of her 2011 film *Kindness Boomerang*. Her talks and workshops provide the groundwork for lasting change and motivate people to become the best version of themselves so that they can influence the world for good. Her giving spirit and passion in life come from a place of recognizing that she mattered at a young age, allowing her to get herself out of the trenches. "Like a life vest, kindness keeps the world afloat."

Scan for the full episode.

Stories of getting out of a difficult trench is a commonality I know most of us share. Everyone has their own trench story. Once you've identified it, remember that every difficult situation you've lived through may have seemed uncomfortable, impossible to deal with or suffocating to you at the time. You may currently be in a trench. Take comfort in the fact that you won't be there forever. While the trials in the trenches bring us down, looking back on them can help us discover how we would react, teach or lead differently if we were in a similar situation again.

Take some time to reflect on the questions below:
- Have you had those days where you just wanted to throw in the towel?
- What were the extenuating factors that led up to those types of days?
- Did you recognize the trench when you were in it?

- How long did it take for you to recognize you were in a trench?
- When you were in that trench, who did you seek out for help?

Chapter 2
A Helping Hand Out of the Trench

I had decided to return to Norway for the summer to work as a tour guide. I would often do this work between school years while earning my Bachelor's degree there. I started looking for teaching jobs in Norway, knowing I'd be there anyway. Within a few weeks of the end of the school year, I had an interview scheduled with a private high school.

I landed the job at a Waldorf School teaching high school French and English. I was out in the country about an hour's drive from Oslo staying in the student dorm house. I was given a free private room with a bathroom in return for a few supervisory responsibilities. What I didn't realize was how invested the students, their families, and most of the staff were in the Waldorf teaching philosophy. I had read some books on the methodology during the summer after getting the job offer, but I was neither trained nor given any materials or websites to review. I was using my public school teaching methods in my classroom along with the little bit of knowledge I had gained from my reading. The school recruited me to teach, yet avoided explaining what type of pedagogy they wanted me to use. I didn't want to be put in a box; I didn't want to have to teach using only the Waldorf teaching method. I decided I wasn't going to get stuck and left before I even felt like I was in a trench. This left me still searching for my purpose.

Looking back on this experience, and having had many conversations through the years since with a colleague of mine from that school, I realized the school's administration was going through a lot of changes. There was also a lot of animosity among several administrators at the high school and the school's founder and head of school. I think it was due to the staff culture I was stepping into that the administration at the school overlooked the fact I needed to be trained in the Waldorf teaching method.

In the summer of 2005, I received three different offers to teach either French or English as a Second Language in Colorado Springs and Denver. I took the job I felt was the best fit even though it was the furthest drive, over an hour and 15 minutes. I would be trained in International Baccalaureate (IB) and teach multiple levels of French, not just levels one and two as I had taught before. I was excited to work with students who had a solid foundation in the language and who I could help prepare for the IB exam. I thoroughly enjoyed teaching during those years, despite a class that may have been rowdy or given me occasional behavior problems. I connected with the students, and most of them enjoyed my class. This was where I found my purpose for teaching. I had found my why. It was fulfilling to see the students I had guided use their French language skills in speaking opportunities and pursue post-secondary studies in which they would use the language.

Once I was comfortable teaching students their second (or third) language, whether it was English, German, Norwegian or French, I realized I wanted to teach students about the cultures in the countries of their chosen language. I wanted students to be able to use the language in practical settings, in a café dialogue exercise or a project on countries where the language is spoken. Seeing them get excited about using their German or French and experiencing light-bulb-moments about things they had assumed about the structure of the language or cultural aspects was very rewarding.

Over the next few years, I grew professionally by attending professional development (PD) sessions, joining Professional Learning Communities (PLCs), and learning from more experienced teachers. I remember, from my first few years of teaching, the students I impacted and the classes that were fun to teach. The most difficult classes I encountered were usually after lunch or when there were 30 or more students in a beginning French class. I slowly shifted my mindset from the "know it all" (fixed mindset) perspective (just because I knew my subject material did not make me a master teacher) to the "growing and evolving" (growth mindset) type of teacher.

The timeline I mapped out in my head for my career transitions didn't always align with what was actually going on in my life. I had to learn to be patient. I went through many seasons of applications, interviews, and rejections. Despite setbacks, I learned how to better prepare myself for school leadership while still working in my teaching position. I continued to develop my skills by consuming all the information that was available to me through digital media, conferences, and district professional development. I learned to tap into resources from others and share their knowledge with those who could benefit from it. I had to reexamine my why several times over the course of my career when my best-laid plans and hopes didn't work out how I wanted them to. I had to come to terms with the fact that each new position or situation within a job was a means of preparing me for the next one.

Here is an example that may be similar to a situation you've experienced. You're a 5th grade teacher who has worked at the same school for seven years. You have been through a few changes in administrative teams and grade-level colleagues. You have attended professional developments for several years, but you don't always implement what you have learned in your practice. Perhaps you don't feel the PD you receive at your school or district is always relevant. For the past school year or so, you may have really started to reevaluate your why. You discover your reason for wanting to be an elementary school teacher has changed since you got into the field of teaching. You start exploring colleges to continue your education and get a graduate degree. You start looking at other ways to serve in the field of education, such as at the district level or as a consultant. The next year, an instructional coach position opens in your district. You view this as a perfect opportunity to use your experience from the classroom to pass those skills along to others who are looking for new and innovative ways to engage their students. While pondering whether to apply to this position, ask yourself if instructional coaching aligns with your why. Sometimes, it takes doing something outside of what you have always done to be connected with your purpose.

Dr. Mechele Newell teaches middle school math, science, and mathematical coding. She is also a girls' basketball coach, change agent, advocate for under-represented/underprivileged youth and a leader in her local ministry in the Bay Area. Her purpose has evolved a few different times over the course of her career so far. She spent time in the Air Force as a clinical laboratory scientist. While she was enlisted, one of her senior leaders asked her to do some didactic training, which is, essentially, teaching in the classroom. She had never really considered it to be her thing, but she loved teaching on the job in the laboratory and decided she would try it out. It was amazing. After she separated from the Air Force, she worked as a post-secondary educator at a vocational school for lab assistants, phlebotomists and EKG techs in Sacramento.

Scan for the full episode.

During her personal time, she coached JV girls' basketball at a local high school that had an International Baccalaureate program. Often, this type of program includes very few Black and Brown students. The school recruited students who came from traditionally "good schools" with high academics to be a part of the Baccalaureate program. Students were also recruited from the local neighborhood, which was located in an area that did not have the highest socioeconomic bracket. The school had a very diverse group of kids. As a coach, she got to meet a lot of young people and learned a lot about their personal lives. Mechele felt some of them could make it playing sports and go to college. She really wanted to help them keep their grades up because a certain level of grades was required for them to be able to play. However, the response she got from teachers was apathetic at best. Many of them felt the students were not going to college anyway, so why bother? She wanted to make an impact with those students that were not being supported. Mechele felt she could make much more of an impact by pursuing K-12 teaching. She realized that she could serve students of color in a community that wasn't helping them reach their full potential.

Mechele's original plan had been to teach middle school science. Unfortunately, she ended up not having the credentials to teach at the secondary level, but she did find out she could teach elementary school. She ended up taking substitute teaching positions for a bit, including one in a 3rd grade classroom. At the end of that day, she told the administration she would substitute in that class again. She could tell the students needed the stability of having the same teacher each day. After that, it was her classroom. Even though 3rd grade wasn't where she had originally imagined herself, she found her niche working with this age group. Sometimes, a trench can lead you down a path you would never have traveled.

Finding purpose while working through a difficult situation, allowed Jim Sporleder to see the potential in his students as well as himself. When he arrived at Lincoln High School in Walla Walla, WA as principal, he couldn't believe the disregard for authority. Gangs basically ruled the school. His goal was to create a safe environment and

Scan for the full episode.

culture. At first, the students didn't like the rules he created. It was about four or five months until the students realized he was there to promote them instead of punish or degrade them. While attending a conference around the end of his third year at Lincoln, he learned about Adverse Childhood Experiences (ACEs): traumatic events such as abuse, neglect, and houschold challenges occurring in a child's life before the age of 18 that can interfere with the child's health and opportunities. He came back and asked his staff to focus on their relationships with the students and change their approach when speaking with kids. Suspension rates dropped drastically each year after that, and discipline numbers continued to decrease.

Discovering that this was the kind of school he was meant to work at opened Jim's eyes. The students at Lincoln High School were in desperate need of a total overhaul of school culture. Implementing trauma-informed practices was the solution to the discipline issues Lincoln was facing and it changed the students' lives for the better.

Under Jim's leadership, Lincoln High School became a Trauma-Informed school. They gained national attention with the significant drop in the number of out-of-school suspensions issued, increased graduation rates and an increase in the number of students going on to post-secondary education. These dramatic changes at Lincoln caught the attention of Jamie Redford, who spent a year filming the documentary, *Paper Tigers*, which tells the Lincoln High School story.

If you don't already know your purpose, your why, finding it can be a challenge. But finding it will definitely clear the way ahead to get out of the trench. On your own, it can be difficult to find your path and stay on it. At times, you may need a little help or guidance. In both personal and professional growth, having an accountability partner is important. Your accountability partner will make sure you're doing what you need to do to build your professional growth plan and reach your goals. This can be a colleague, friend, coach, family member or spouse. Think about who you have in your life that could hold you accountable for completing your daily goals, be it practicing mindfulness or meditation, getting enough rest and relaxation, exercise, journaling, or whatever else you have as part of your day-to-day schedule.

For example, if you are trying to build your personal professional development plan for the school year, you could consider getting insight from your accountability partner. They can also help you stay on track with your plan and remind you to use the skills you've learned from your PD sessions and share them with other educators in your building.

When was the last time you updated your résumé? If you haven't looked for a new position recently, have you at least updated the skills you've been acquiring all this time? Whether or not you've recently changed roles, you have likely gained many skills you didn't have before. Don't be frustrated if you haven't used the skills you listed on your five-year-old résumé since that time. What skills do you have right now that are transferable from your current position to another one (even if you can't even think of ever leaving your current job)? For example, I transferred the public speaking skills I gained in college guiding tourists through the city of Tromsø, Norway to speaking in front of a classroom full of students.

As an educator, you're a life-long learner, and whatever trench you're currently experiencing is giving you tools to help you further down the line. Those moments you are living in the trench will be those you reflect on later if a similar situation crops up. I highly recommend the practice of journaling or blogging. If I could have read some of my reflections from back then, and how I look at things now from an older, wiser perspective, it would have given me a wealth of information. Everyone's story is different as is their way out of the trenches. What are some of your resources you could use to pull yourself out of the trench?

Perhaps you have not found where you fit yet. You may have been in many schools and spent only a short period in each because they never seemed to be the right fit. If that is your situation, consider these questions:
- Have you identified your dream school? If you are looking at making a career move, how do the schools you're applying to fit the description of the dream school you're looking for?
- How can you build your resources in the trenches before you start climbing out?
- Have you dug deeper into the skills you need to keep up with today's educational demands and considered any additional education or training?

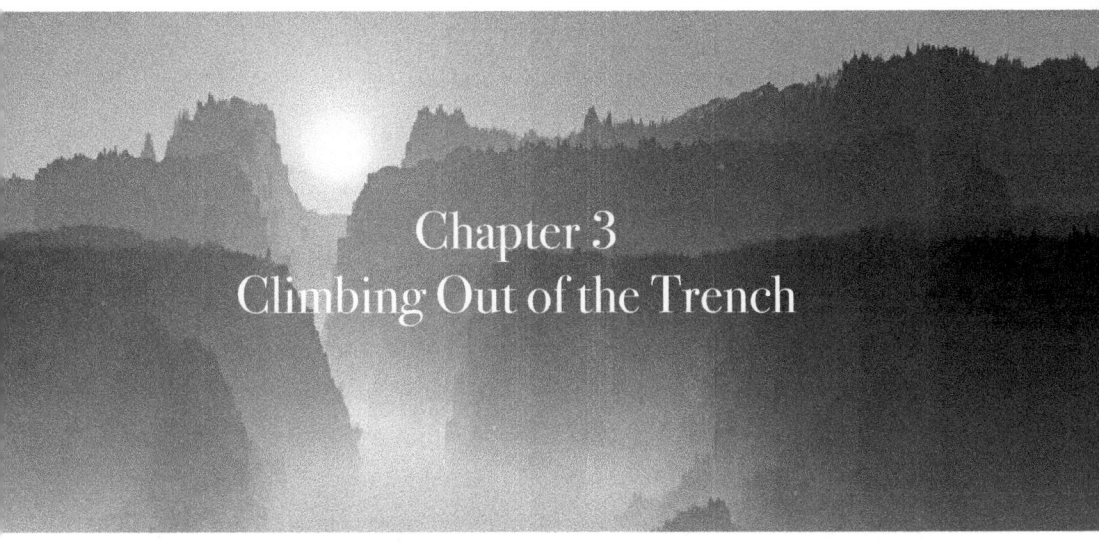

Chapter 3
Climbing Out of the Trench

After nine years in education, I realized my educational why had shifted. In a guest blog post I wrote for Teach Better Team on March 4, 2021, *Be a Leader Who Empowers Your Staff*, I explained that I was given the chance to get into teacher leadership positions early in my teaching career. I was appointed to the position of department chair for World Languages for the first time in 2006, about four years into my K-12 teaching journey. I hadn't asked for the extra responsibility or leadership position, but when the previous chair left, I was the second in seniority and the first choice to be the next department chair. What I learned that year about leading a department and being a part of the Instructional Leadership Team at a large high school helped propel my desire to become a school leader.

I have also been a part of the attendance team at three different high schools, as well as helped to form a parent partners coalition at one of those schools. Parental involvement is a topic that I have always been passionate about, especially at the secondary school level. As a result of these experiences, my desire to become a school leader was growing stronger and stronger by the year.

For me, getting into school administration wasn't a one-and-done deal. I took my first course in the principal licensure program in the spring of 2005 but didn't continue with the next session. It wasn't a wise financial choice for me to pursue any more coursework at the time. I picked up the program again in 2009 and completed it two years later, all while having my first two kids in spring 2008 and early 2010. I knew that school leadership was the direction I wanted to pursue, I just didn't fully understand or value the need to make connections and network while doing my internship for the program. Looking back, I realize this affected me in that I didn't know how to network within the schools where I interned. I didn't know how to connect with the right people who might have been in a position to offer me a dean or assistant principal (AP) position.

Thus, despite applying for leadership positions starting in 2011, I spent several more years in the classroom, honing my skills, participating in PLCs, and building relationships with students and stakeholders. When I was finally given the opportunity to break into school administration, I was offered a dean position about one hour's commute from my home. Although the commute was long and the school was tough (a Title I middle school with many ongoing school culture issues), I knew I needed this experience to move to the next level. I would definitely say that this was a deep trench for me in terms of the commute and the demands of the job.

I was excited to finally work on an administrative team, to share my experiences and learn from the other APs and the principal. I oversaw all of the discipline and attendance in the school, with a population of around 600 students. To give some data about this experience, the end-of-year count for suspensions was 420 (many for the same students). The number of students expelled by the end of the year was 14. I wrote attendance plans for 148 students, and I went to district truancy hearings (student review board) for about 20 kids in March and April. These were required for students who had 25-40 days of absences during the year. The school tried using a teen court model. This led to a reduction in out-of-school suspensions by giving alternative consequences but had mixed results, depending on the student. Although I only stayed at that school for a year, I gained a great deal of knowledge in how to communicate with families, stakeholders and, especially, how to listen when meeting with an upset student or parent. While this experience was what I labeled "trial under fire," it cemented my desire to make a difference in the lives of students and to help them and their families seek out resources in the community. It also taught me A TON about school culture and how to transform it as a leader. This experience impacted me and my leadership by reshaping how I wanted to lead.

Using your tools and resources to make changes in your life can help you get out of the trenches. Consider if the resources from the previous chapter along with the ones coming up could help you out.

As well as being a podcast host, I have been a guest on many podcasts. In April 2021, I was a guest on Ann Hlabangana-Clay's podcast, *Coaching You Through All Things Education*. In this episode, I spoke about partnering with parents and getting professional development within your building. Using a professional day to have teachers learn from each other gives teachers an opportunity to feel more connected to the school. For secondary teachers going into a different content area, seeing strategies from their own school building's talent of how to present the content can be extremely helpful. It's one key to positive culture if there is a willingness to share with colleagues within your building.

I also spoke with Ann about my EdD research into parents opting out of the state's high stakes test. For many years, some teachers in subject areas that are on this test (math, science and English) have taught to the test. Even the state evaluation system rated teachers partly based on how their students performed on this test. Ann and I discussed how the future of high-stakes testing might change. Some colleges aren't using the SAT as an admission requirement, reflecting the knowledge of what's best for kids. The last question Ann asked me was which legacy message I would put on a billboard. I answered with, "Don't hold back, go for things you want to pursue in order to accomplish greater things." I referred to Brandon Beck's thoughts in his book, *Unlocking Unlimited Potential*. Everyone has potential for greatness, we just need to discover what that potential is. Go after what you want without making excuses.

Making a professional development plan for yourself, and following it, will keep you moving forward in your career and in your life. Keep these questions in mind when you are planning your individual professional development plan for the year:

- How do you filter through the wide array of PD offerings available to you?
- What are the best PD options for you and your team this upcoming school year (virtual, in-person in your building, book clubs or book study, etc.)?
- How can *you* be proactive in starting book studies and other staff opportunities based on the PD you have participated in?
- What authors in the field of current educational innovation should you be reading and perhaps leading book clubs on?
- Which podcasts for educators should you be listening to?
- What kind of webinars would you like to attend and how often, or what district PD offerings would you like to sign up for?
- Are you the type of educator who needs check-ins regarding the progression of your yearly PD journey?
- If you have received school funds for part of your professional development, do you need to report back to your grade-level team or department on what you learned at the conference?
- How do you grow when no one's leading professional growth?
- How do you know what you need to learn to grow professionally?
- How do you get beyond "good enough" when you're trying to grow?

Danna Thomas runs Happy Teacher Revolution, an organization that it's an international movement on a mission to transform the lives of educators by empowering them to claim happiness as their own. Her way of supporting teachers to get out of the trenches is to have them set goals around the important message that we all have the power and action over our own choices, even though it might not always feel like something we're motivated to follow through on.

For some educators, the road to success isn't always straight; it can take many twists and turns. Setting goals, short- and long-term, are imperative to keeping you on track, professionally and personally. When it comes to goal setting you might consider the following questions/statements:

- What could I do today that will help me get closer to my monthly, quarterly, or yearly goals?
- What could I do differently today/this week to help me reach my goals?
- How can I adjust my behavior moving forward to help me reach my goals?
- In the past, how did you find PD that worked best for your learning styles and professional goals for the year?
- With your department (or as an individual), develop a PD plan that will fit your professional needs.
- If you're a school leader, evaluate what you included in your yearly PD plan and seek to include a more encompassing professional development for the next school year.
- Your end goal statement should be: "Here's where I need to grow, here's what will inspire me to keep growing."

Sometimes, as teachers and leaders who often want full control of our environment, we want to do all those busy work tasks ourselves such as filing papers, setting up for activities, and sending email reminders. Some of these tasks can easily be delegated to student assistants if you're a teacher or to the administrative assistant if you're in school leadership. I have learned quite a bit about delegating tasks and spending less time on office tasks by using resources from Danny Bauer of Better Leaders, Better Schools and from Justin Baeder of The Principal Center. Justin's Inbox Overhaul, for example, is a mini-course that helps leaders get through their inbox faster. He also offers another mini-course on Systems for Office Effectiveness that includes delegating tasks and which tasks need to be completed by you.

As a teacher, I was often the type of person who felt like they didn't have much for a student assistant to do. I felt like it was more work than it needed to be to plan things for the assistant to complete. During my first year as an administrator, I worked hard to complete district-mandated attendance plans for an increasing number of habitually truant students. Being new to the building and district, I was not sure how to go about completing these many plans before the deadline. I had formed an attendance committee at the school, but there was not much interest from the staff to be involved as there was already a longer-than-usual school day due to it being a Title I school. Eventually, several administrative assistants, myself, and a few other staff members who weren't in the classroom volunteered regularly to help interview students for the attendance plans. Delegating tasks, for me, led to some difficulty when I first tried. Eventually, with the help of these staff members, I found my groove, and we were able to complete the task at hand.

A couple of tips for delegating: make a list of tasks that need to be completed ahead of time and work towards goals incrementally. Set up a schedule or list of tasks for those you're delegating to so they can check tasks off as they are completed.

Frank Buck is a former band teacher and school administrator, speaker, and author of three books. He has shown countless professionals an easier way to work. Through his workshops, books, and coaching, Dr. Buck shares these secrets with leaders about how practical and easy it can be to get organized. Frank was in the trenches during his first-year teaching when he accepted a mid-year middle school band director opening. A snowstorm hit the week after he started, closing the school for a week. Frank had only six weeks after his first day to prepare his students for a big band concert. Despite his school being closed, Frank came up to the school every day to plan.

Scan for the full episode.

Having hammered out those concert plans during the weather closure proved very effective, enabling him to recycle the plans later. Tools such as recording his lessons helped him hone his teaching skills over the year and self-correct. He explained that by using lesson recordings you can find verbal tics, that you're only teaching to one side of the room, or whispered conversations that took place in the back of the classroom that you weren't aware of before you viewed the video.

Frank's book, *Get Organized, Digitally!: The Educator's Guide to Time Management,* looks at the digital part of getting organized. In it, he references seven things people can look for when entering tasks into a digital task list. He points out that many of these tools are especially useful to new principals. They spend so much time their first year trying to run the building themselves (the management piece), instead of focusing more on instructional leadership (the leadership piece). When you start to make choices about tasks, you can delegate the things that take a lot of managerial time to parents, students, and administrative assistants such as student-led announcements, bulletin boards, newsletters, social media posts, and much more. Life doesn't have to be as hard as we sometimes make it. Don't feel overwhelmed.

The resources you use may help you through one trench, but you might need to find other resources to dig out of your next trench. For me, speaking at conferences has been a great resource. Not only do I get to share my expertise, I am able to learn from others by attending the conference. You may want to work with a professional coach to work through some challenges within your school or district. You could join a cohort of other educators, such as an online book club or mastermind, to discuss challenges with a group outside your school or district. Take some time now to jot down some ideas of what you could start (or continue) doing. Don't forget to think big!

Chapter 4
Finding What Makes Your Passion Grow

The summer after leaving the dean of students position, I almost felt as if I had to detox from the negativity I had been dealing with on a day-to-day level there. I reflected on the year that had passed and made the decision that I would lead *transformatively* and *with transparency* and thought about what that would look like. I reflected on what I had contributed and how I could have done better in certain situations. I fell short, sometimes, with my reactions to student and staff behavior. I often had to catch myself and realized I needed to stay in my lane and do only the duties as assigned and not step outside the boundaries of the position. I set goals for myself as a future assistant principal to avoid some of the reactions and mistakes I had experienced during my year of trial under fire. I consumed numerous books on school culture such as *Relentless: Changing Lives by Disrupting the Educational Norm* by Hamish Brewer, *Hacking School Discipline: 9 Ways to Create a Culture of Empathy and Responsibility by Using Restorative Justice* by Nathan Maynard & Brad Weinstein, and *School Culture Recharged: Strategies to Energize Your Staff and Culture* by Todd Whitaker and Matt Grunert.

The way out of the trench, for me, was to move on. I was not hired as a principal who could come in and make sweeping changes. I was hired as a dean, and that school had too many long–standing procedures and staples of negative school culture. I knew I could not grow in a toxic environment.

In the spring of that year, I thought it would be easy to get an assistant principal job with my experience as Dean of Students, but I had to go through many more interviews throughout an extended period of time to actually land one. People don't talk about this because there can be a level of shame involved after you've gone to interview after interview, only to feel like you're just a number or a person who was only interviewed because the hiring team had to meet a quota. In my mind, I can easily go back to times when I thought I had done *everything* possible to knock it out of the park on several job interviews, only to not get a call or email back, or to get a generic: we went in a different direction (don't you love that one?). Sometimes I actually spoke with the principal and received positive, detailed feedback that I couldn't have done any better but that the position had been slated for an internal candidate. I didn't give up, however. I knew why I wanted to become an assistant principal.

Tyson Gardin is an elementary assistant principal in the Chester County School District in Chester, SC. He is passionate about making a positive impact on equity and excellence in schools and encourages students to make their own positive and lasting impact in our world.

Tyson persevered for years in the trench to get an Assistant Principal job. At one point in his career, he decided that he wanted to be an instructional leader. So, he took the required courses and thought he was going to start his administrative journey right away. It took him seven years to land an assistant principal position. He was going through the trials of applying and not getting interviews. He wondered who would take a chance on him? When would he be good enough? He was ready to give up. Luckily, he has a wonderful support system with his family. They helped him decide to give it one more go. He is so glad he did or he wouldn't be where he is today. He learned that he needed those experiences, the interviews and the positions he held, to get him where he is now. Whether you feel like giving up or trudging forward, there is a light at the end of the tunnel.

Scan for the full episode.

In October of 2021, Dr. Rosa Perez-Isiah was a guest on Principal Kafele's *Virtual Assistant Principal Leadership Academy* broadcast. Kafele asked what Dr. Perez-Isiah would say to someone who is constantly facing closed doors. Her response was, "It will happen, your time will come." Educators must continually practice patience and foster resilience within themselves. When there are disappointments and setbacks, it can cause worry, hopelessness, and helplessness. Believe me, there are going to be times when you feel like you have done everything possible and are not making any headway. I am here to tell you – don't give up on what you've worked so hard for. There is a place out there for you to make a difference working with students and staff!

Dr. Sarah Thomas came to the field of teaching from a radio/tv background after stumbling upon a flier advertising a teacher position. From there, she participated in a summer session that gave her some pedagogical foundations. She was young and impatient at the time, and instead of waiting for schools to reach out to her and find a good fit, she decided to venture out and make her own connections. Dr. Thomas ended up teaching at three schools in four years, none of the first three were a good fit for her. Things started to get better at the fourth school. She had a principal who saw leadership capacity in her and put her in a leadership role for the very first time. That started to repair the way she saw herself. She didn't have very high self-esteem when it came to her teaching abilities as a result of those first few rocky years. The principal trusted her to do what she could and to use her strengths to help all the students in the building as well as the educators. She really felt like she was part of something. Then, she started working with the district tech team. She began to connect with other educators through Twitter and found her Professional Learning Network (PLN). It was all because she was in a space where she felt comfortable taking those small risks to improve herself and improve her practice.

Scan for the full episode.

The leaders she worked with helped her see herself as a leader. Dr. Thomas went on to find her passion working on the regional tech team. She also started EduMatch in 2014, first as a place for educators to connect on Twitter, then as an educational publishing company.

Dr. Thomas' story is not that uncommon. Many educators have started their careers going from building to building, trying to find the right fit, often not getting support, but not giving up on their dreams of becoming a successful teacher. It takes persistence and determination.

Danny Bauer is the founder of *Better Leaders, Better Schools*, a podcast host, and author of the *The Better Leaders Better Schools Roadmap: Small Ideas that Lead to Big Impact* and *Mastermind: Unlocking Talent Within Every School Leader.* Danny provides coaching to leaders, or as he calls them "ruckus makers," to bring them out of the isolation that is often found in school leadership to help them level up their leadership. During his last principalship, he went from everything going great to getting written up for the first time in his career within a week's time. It went from "we're so excited you're here" to "we have serious concerns about your leadership." Stakeholders in the community were making positive comments on social media, but the district leadership was saying the opposite. Looking back, he appreciated that he used a gratitude journal, mindfulness practices, meditation, and the mastermind he's been a part of since 2015 as resources to help him out of that trench. Danny reminds us that people should give themselves some grace when they're going through a tough time in the trench. We need to remember we don't need to have it all figured out. If you have the community and solid routines and rituals, these can help give you

Scan for the full episode.

time out of that trench. Instead of wallowing in self-pity, Danny built upon what he had already started and grew his Better Leaders Better Schools mindset into an organization, touching the lives of principals worldwide. Danny's passion for growing and supporting school leaders demonstrates the potential for others interested in facilitating professional learning or other facets of educational growth.

Most educators with some level of experience can lead professional development. If you're an undergraduate student, think of it as the presentations you give to your classmates. If you're a new teacher, think of the student projects and essays they write. If you're a member of a professional organization, there are usually one to two conferences a year looking for proposal submissions from presenters. There are different ways to go about creating, proposing, preparing, and presenting PD for a small or large group. Often, any given session has a pair or panel of presenters, so you don't have to do it alone! Take a moment to think about local, state, or national conferences you have attended in the past or would like to attend soon and would like to submit a proposal to.

Whether you've been in the classroom for a few years or are in a teacher prep program, you can seek out opportunities to share your experiences and expertise at conference breakout sessions or during in-service PD days at your school. When you get your feet wet speaking to your peers at an in-building PD, it becomes easier to speak to larger groups in breakout sessions at conferences.

The first time I led a PD session, I was roughly eight years into the teaching profession and new to the school and district where I was working. It was a district PD day, and we met with subject-area colleagues. Leading up to this day, there was a request for ideas for sessions. The presentation I gave was about being a National Endowment for the Humanities grant recipient the summer before and how my experience shaped my teaching practice. While this presentation didn't have a huge audience, I was happy with the turnout and the opportunity to present and share my experience. However, I didn't present again for almost ten years!

I started to become more interested in speaking at conferences in 2017 while attending a train-the-trainer, four-day workshop. The workshop was about teacher break-out sessions on student engagement and classroom management. I used these resources for several years to lead break-out sessions on this subject at local, state, and regional conferences. This turned into a passion of mine. I got a rush of excitement presenting to large audiences and sharing my expertise. I learned how to read an audience and to know when to adjust presentations for length and to add or subtract activities, like one does in a classroom. I get the chance to connect with other educators during and after breakout sessions. I appreciate hearing questions and receiving comments from those in the classroom who are struggling. I enjoy being able to point them in a direction to seek more resources or start a committee in their building.

I realized that I needed to expand my presentations beyond the classroom management and student engagement aspect. I started writing a session on Finding Your PD Niche and realized that I could still speak on student engagement but align it to equitable practices using social-emotional teaching strategies. That presentation evolved into managing classroom discipline issues post-pandemic and the challenges teachers faced after students returned to brick-and-mortar classrooms.

If you are considering speaking professionally, start locally. Apply to speak at conferences and professional events, they all have a call for proposals before the conference takes place. Building a spreadsheet with the list of conferences and their proposal deadlines is a great way to keep you organized. You don't need to have speaking experience to submit a proposal, but you do need to be able to write a comprehensive proposal of what your breakout session will be about. Most submissions require at least a list of objectives for participants and a session summary. Other organizations may require much more, such as the alignment of your proposal to the organization's or state's standards. Expect to spend between 20-45 minutes on each proposal if you're just starting out. Also, there is a good chance you will not be paid to speak at the conference and you will need to pay your way. Some conferences offer a presenter discount but not all, and the discount offered is, oftentimes, not much. So, when you're ready to develop a presentation, you can do this yourself or bring a colleague on board. Find a list of conferences you'd like to present at, and make sure you take note of the registration fee before you apply to speak. This way you won't be caught off guard by being accepted to speak at a conference you can't afford to attend.

You may not be interested in actually developing or leading professional development. Your passion may lie elsewhere. Think of areas you may be able to branch out and expand your horizons.

In episode 75 of *Virtual Assistant Principal Leadership Academy* broadcast, Principal Kafele noted that many educators need to think about areas where they should pivot. We can't be the same educator we were when we first started in our careers. Educators should be learning, growing and continually reinventing themselves in their current or subsequent roles. Sometimes this means leaving the role you are in for something new.

As you can see, I have been in the trenches from time to time, but life is what we make it. Don't stay too long at a school that is not the right fit or hang around colleagues who make you unhappy. As a professional, you must decide when it is your time to leave. We have all been there. It may be a series of bad days, a repeating list of grievances about the district or school you work in, or it may be an opportunity you can't pass up that leads to your departure. Whatever the situation may be, weigh your pros and cons. Some people want to have a new job lined up before they leave their current one. Others I have known don't know what their next move may be at the end of the school year, but they are leaving regardless. A former social studies teacher colleague of mine became a yoga instructor after leaving teaching when she just couldn't take it anymore. I'm not suggesting a total life overhaul is necessary, but there may come a time in your life when you will have to decide: *Do I stay or do I leave?*

Use the following questions to help you find and follow your passion:.
- How can you find what makes your passion grow?
- How do you set professional goals for yourself every year?
- How have your professional goals changed over the course of your career?
- Who can you discuss your goals with?
- Are you setting both personal and professional goals?

- Which goals do you find it hardest to meet and why?

Chapter 5
Keeping Yourself Out of the Trenches

Before the beginning of the 2021-2022 school year, I attended a back-to-school, district-wide professional development in which the facilitator talked about working your way inward from your why to your what, then finding out the how. The facilitator referenced Simon Sinek's TedX 2009 video in which he explains why some people achieve things easier than others. In Sinek's Golden Circle, Why is in the center circle, How is in the middle circle, and What is in the outer circle. Inspired organizations think and act from the inside out. What is your why and how has that changed in the past couple of years? Can you define your why at this stage in your career?

If you're navigating challenges in your role and need to reconsider your why, take time to reevaluate your purpose in education.

Whatever you choose to do as a next step, know that everything you have learned from your experiences has shaped you. You have skills that can transfer to many roles in and outside of education. I reevaluated my purpose in 2009-2010 when, due to budget restraints surrounding world language teaching positions, I was unemployed. Thus, I went to the local workforce center to take some assessments and see what skills I had that could transfer to other roles. I wasn't necessarily considering an alternate career outside of education, but I completed these assessments to get a picture of how I could use my skills from classroom teaching in other roles working with students and families. What are some transferable skills you have that you use in daily life, or in another job you may have?

Many teachers go into a Master's program to further their learning and don't always consider whether they're going to use what they learn in those courses. For some, it may be 10 or more years before they use their Master's in school administration, instructional coaching, or a district curriculum developer position. In Rob Breyer's book, *Taking the Leap: A Field Guide for Aspiring School Leaders,* he explains that persistence pays off when you're applying to next-level positions. Whether you're aspiring to become a department chair, school leader, superintendent, or district-level administrator, your goals can be achieved if you work hard at them. Rob's field guide is a way for candidates to explore areas in which they may need some practice, whether it be résumé review, cover letter writing, or interviewing. Having many versions of résumés and cover letters throughout the years is not only a tool to build upon, but it allows you to highlight your skills and experiences gained through the years.

Some templates or strategies for educators that I have found helpful are from Justin Baeder and the Principal Center's Ascend program. He recommends interview strategies, email correspondence dos and don'ts, résumé development, the ability to speak to the résumé, and the ability to consolidate information in an interview. Justin also hosts live webinars on the school leader interview process.

Karine Veldhoen, of Learn Forward, created a school leadership self-assessment tool based on her evaluations, work she did in her province, and a few other tools she researched. She made it her own based on the five pillars of school leadership. According to Karine, school leaders should be intentional about completing their own self-assessment and transitioning it into a professional growth plan that they own and direct. Too often in education, we're waiting for someone else to provide or guide us, rather than designing and pursuing our professional learning. Self-evaluation is important for growth, personally and professionally.

During a typical school year, many educators only devote the months of May and June for self-reflection, since that is a natural point in the school year when they're wrapping up. Why not reflect at the end of quarters or months or right before a school break? Build-in more time to discover how much you can shift your practice, renew your outlook and adjust your approach to your work. Tools and actionable strategies that are simple, easy to use, and quick to apply are learned by discovering what makes your passions grow. It may or may not be tied to your work in education. What types of activities fill your bucket? What can you do to dig yourself out of the trenches, if you are deep in them?

Steven Gupton is a Career & Technical Education (CTE) teacher at James E. Shepard IB Magnet Middle School in Durham Public Schools. In high school, he began volunteering in his local fire department and his love for public service began to grow. He walked away from his role as an EMS administrator to join the teaching profession and he's glad he did. Steven reminds us not to let our past experiences define us. He combined his passion for CTE and EMS into his drive to teach students so they can explore a future career as an EMS administrator. He credits his former teachers who saw the drive and passion he already had in middle school. He is now becoming that teacher who is recognizing that drive in his own students today.

Scan for the full episode.

Jessica Johnson is an author, speaker and superintendent in Wisconsin. She is a co-author of *The Coach Approach: Leading Teachers to Higher Levels of Effectiveness* and *Balance like a Pirate: Going Beyond Work-Life Balance to Ignite Passion and Thrive as an Educator*, and co-moderator of the PrincipalPLN podcast. At one point in her life, Jessica neglected her basic self-care needs for years. She ignored mild symptoms until they became bigger issues. It took her many wake-up calls to understand she was not balancing her work and personal life. She realized she needed to make her life better, but it wasn't necessarily a job change that would lead her down the right path. She focuses on helping other educators take time to put themselves first. Jessica makes a point to check in with her teachers and ask what she can do to help support them and have

Scan for the full episode.

grace for them. She believes that self-care isn't selfish, because when you're healthy you can better serve your students.

Educator burnout is nothing new but became much more prevalent during the pandemic. The signs of burnout can be subtle or loud, and it's up to the individual to recognize that something must be done to get help or change habits of overwork before it's too late. Symptoms of compassion fatigue and empathy burnout can show up in many ways. It's important to know when you need to take a break to rest, recover and recoup.

Some strategies and resources to keep you out of the trenches do not always directly affect you. Using these types of resources may be the most helpful in the long run to keep you out of the trenches. As an educator, you are a leader of the opportunities and responsibilities that may guide students and families. Sometimes, by helping others, you are helping yourself.

Student Leadership Opportunities
By providing students opportunities to lead at your school, you give them ways to strengthen their character. This will, in turn, be reflected in their behavior in the classroom. If they are often disruptive and you provide them with student leadership opportunities, they will realize this potential in themselves. If you're feeling like you're in the trenches due to challenges with classroom management, identify students who have personality traits that may fit well with student leadership opportunities. This will help them cultivate their strengths and use something to support other students that may have otherwise manifested as a classroom disruption.

Support from the Community
In working with students and their families, as both a teacher and an administrator, I have found that students attending a high-needs school often do not have the best environment at home or in their neighborhood. Many of these students can benefit from after-school clubs and activities such as the YMCA or the Boys and Girls Club of America. If your job in any way involves working towards student success outcomes (which is really all of us), it is worthwhile to discover community organizations in your area that can help support students. Don't be afraid to reach out and forge a partnership with them. They are usually more than willing and ready to help provide things such as mentors, help with canned goods and coat drives, and work with your school to provide after-school mentoring and activity opportunities.

How our students are doing in their home lives often affects us and can, sometimes, keep us up at night. When you reach out to community organizations, you're ensuring your students are supported when they leave your building. Community partnerships can indirectly help you work your way out of a trench by helping you connect with students and families in a way that will positively impact both you and the families you serve.

Building Relationships with Stakeholders
Building relationships is an important aspect of keeping yourself out of the trenches, or getting yourself out if you are already in one. When you maintain positive, communicative relationships with all stakeholders, you are alleviating a big reason for some of us to slide into the trenches. Keeping open lines of communication, that go both ways, will just be one less thing to keep you down.

Maybe you have parents who don't understand the school culture, expectations for attendance or grading policies. Maybe they are not getting as much information from the teacher or school as they'd hoped. You can avoid a conflict by ensuring your school's website and social media pages are up to date. If your teachers have their own webpages or social media, make sure they are keeping their pages up to date with information about assignments, due dates, resources and grading policies. Phone calls, texts and emails are also beneficial lines of communication.

Unfortunately, some communications with stakeholders may not always be positive. If you have received a phone call, text or email from an upset parent, it's important to acknowledge that they are upset for a reason. Your first impulse may be to defend yourself, your school or your teacher. Instead, listen calmly, gather all the information you will need to investigate the complaint and maintain professional boundaries. Let the parent know you'll be following up with them shortly on their concerns. Within the next 24 hours, come up with a solution, and if there is no immediate solution, give them steps you will follow to assist them. While the way you approach a situation varies greatly, you may want to enlist the help of those who have experienced a similar situation. Finally, don't take the negative communication personally.

Empowering Families
Parents want what is best for their children but don't always know where to start or how to access helpful resources. Even at the secondary level, we want to let parents know that they are partners with the school because we're all working towards the goal of helping our students succeed. Some parents may initially be

resistant to getting help from the school because of their previous experience with school staff. If you are working to gain the support of parents and guardians, don't hesitate to ask clarifying questions to learn more about them, their students, and their family life situation.

As educators, and for those of us who are also parents, we sometimes feel like we're in the trenches when we encounter a situation with a student that seems insurmountable. When we're able to forge a connection with families of children who really need our support, we form a team with them. We show we truly care by listening to them and offering help in finding solutions. This will do a lot to keep us out of the trenches by keeping relationships with parents and guardians positive and proactive.

It may be that the resources that keep us out of the trenches are the things we don't necessarily equate to being a resource at all. Self-care can never be emphasized enough. I am one of those people who thrive while multitasking. I am always listening to podcasts and vodcasts on educational topics while I write, check emails and plan my work. However, constantly having a voice in my ear and being in front of the computer can wear me down. I have a Fitbit that reminds me to get up and move every hour, but I admit that sometimes I ignore the reminder if I am in the middle of something. I still make sure to get a fresh start each morning by getting up about a half-hour before anyone else in the house (except for the dog, who usually wakes me up). I spend those minutes listening to the Calm© app and stretching. I make sure I get about one hour of exercise daily, preferably early in the morning. During the school day, for the past eight years, I have made it a point to walk around the building, the school track, or neighborhood streets for about 20 minutes. These moments of solitude and reflection pay off in giving me more energy to complete tasks, being able to parent effectively when my kids get home and trying to remain a positive presence around my husband when conflict arises, as it inevitably does in life. For example, to work on the manuscript of this book, I took a weekend away from my husband and three kids at a hotel to be able to fully concentrate on the writing. From that experience, I realized the benefits of taking time away to focus deeply on projects.

When the going gets tough in the trenches, who do you tend to reach out to? Do you have friends, colleagues, or family members who can support you in doing what you need to implement and practice self-care daily? Too often, educators say there are not enough hours in the day to practice self-care. If you don't take the time to intentionally implement and practice daily self-care, it will not happen; no one will do it for you. *You* are responsible for your schedule, and *your* decisions affect your attitude while you serve students in your daily work. In her article "Top 10 Rules for Self-Love," Brené Brown talks about having both gratitude and joy. We, as a civilization, struggle with believing we're enough. We receive messages that fuel the sense of imperfection and us not being worthy of belonging and joy. Brené says, "Vulnerability is the number one casualty of a scarcity culture." Her advice is to let go of your armor, trauma, or insecurities you may be carrying from childhood. She also urges us to let go of perfectionism. Perfectionism is a way of saying, *if I look perfect, act perfect, I can avoid blame and criticism.* If you always worry about what people will think, you can never do anything brave. Taking risks as an educator requires bravery. Stop comparing yourself to the teacher down the hall. Your journey looks totally different than theirs. Be vulnerable and discover new ways of taking care of yourself. You'll be less reactive to those around you, and you'll thank yourself for it down the road. Through my own lens, and those of some of the leaders I have interviewed, I have discussed self-love and learning to be enough in the workplace. Educators must balance a lot and we wear many hats. It's hard to even see the top of the trenches sometimes.

As Jen Molitor shares in her book, *The Happy Teacher's Handbook: From Overwhelmed to Inspired–Helping Teachers Embrace Resiliency*, sometimes spreading yourself too thin will catch up with you, as it did with her when she had to take three weeks off for asthmatic bronchitis. She states, "When we run at that pace, every day, we lose sight of what balance looks like. We forget what it's like to spend quality time with our kids or husband or ourselves. We forget that when we run out of energy, we have nothing more to give and everyone loses." As Jessica Cabeen wrote in *Leading with Grace: Leaning into the Soft Skills of Leadership (Lead Forward)*, "Leading with grace and vulnerability means that sometimes we need to ask for help and support through the dark challenges and seasons of our personal lives. (...) Regardless of the duration of the storm, finding ways to ask for help and seeking care for yourself is essential to walk through the storm with the confidence necessary to survive."

You may discover that taking time for self-care is essential for you to find that balance between work and home life. For me, decompressing is my daily 15-20 minute walk to get fresh air and clear my head. For some, decompressing may be listening to podcasts while running or journaling about experiences from which we have learned. I have used a leadership journal for several years. Consider starting a gratitude journal to record three things you're grateful for every day.

This chapter has included a wealth of different thoughts and considerations for educators who are looking for inspiration on how to keep themselves out of the trenches. Whether your path is similar to any of the stories mentioned or vastly different, my goal with this part of the book is to help you remember that we all go through difficulties and changes during our careers. Everyone has encountered them (no matter how successful they are). You may dip into the trenches again from time to time after you've gotten out of huge trenches, but your way of dealing with the situation will change in how you react to it.

Learning from others and reflecting on your practice from year to year is easy for some, harder for others. Write down some ways you have learned from those around you, both from those in your building and those you're connected to online.

Chapter 6
Thriving in the Trenches

Although I interpret the term trenches to mean going through a challenging time, many people feel the trenches are where they thrive. They don't find it a hardship to get in there and do the hard work. They look for ways to support staff and really understand what fires teachers up about their teaching and what fires students up about learning. They seek new ways for educators within their realm of influence to work effectively with kids. As you read the following stories, think of trenches you have walked through that turned out to be a positive experience for you.

Dr. Danny Brassell has held a variety of titles and worked with leaders from a variety of fields and disciplines, but he has always considered himself, first and foremost, a teacher. He is a best-selling author of 16 books, including *Leadership Begins with*

Motivation: 33 Unique Ways to Think & Act Like a Successful Leader That Will Transform Your Professional & Personal Life and *The Reading Makeover*, based on his popular TEDx talk. Danny is a recognized authority on leadership development, reading, motivation, and communication skills as well as the co-creator of the world's top reading engagement program. Danny loves being in the trenches working with kids and helping them learn how to read. Tutoring kids one-on-one taught him how to make an impact with kids. He has worked with countless educators and parents whose kids are excited about reading.

He says, "The question I always ask schools is, what good is it teaching kids how to read if they never want to read? I never want to have to tell a kid to go read a book. I want them to do it because they choose to do it on their own."

Scan for the full episode.

Matt Miller is the superintendent of Lakota Local Schools. He has spent the last 26 years serving Ohio communities. He was selected as one of 100 superintendents nationwide to attend and present at the Future Ready National ConnectED Superintendents' Summit at the White House. He is Lead Advisor for the Future Ready District Leaders' strand and was named to the National School Boards Association's Top 20 to Watch in the Nation. Matt is transforming Lakota through the use of open educational resources and balanced learning, along with emphasizing student and teacher voice through innovation. He approached the implementation of fully in-person learning throughout the 2020-2021 school year in his district with a positive attitude. All the contact tracing, mask mandates, and shifts in instructional models that others may have felt was a trench was where Matt thrived. He encouraged other leaders during that time to collaborate through networks and learn what other schools were doing. He surveyed his community to find out what type of learning model they preferred and stuck to their preferences. He believes in saying yes to teachers when they want to try something innovative. Matt stresses that you must be flexible as a school or district leader; be supportive of what your staff is doing. Don't be afraid of taking risks because the students and staff you serve are depending on you.

Scan for the full episode.

Jami Fowler-White has found herself in the trenches many times throughout the years. At one point, she was substitute teaching at a school in which a teacher quit unexpectedly. The principal went to Jami and asked if she would like to take the second grade long-term substitute position. She was overjoyed to accept. The only hitch was that the principal needed her to start Monday, and the day she accepted the job was Friday. Over the weekend, Jami's family got together to help her get the classroom set up. She was there ten days and was told she had to leave that particular assignment. She was saddened by this as the school was very open and welcoming. She could ask questions of anyone in the building and get help.

With three months left in the school year, she was thrown into a completely different environment about 15 minutes away. The principal got her in for a quick meeting and told Jami not to ask for anything and not to send students to the office. The principal also told Jami she would be the fifth teacher for the second grade class she would be teaching. At the time Jami was at this school, the district was trying out different curricula. This meant there was no specific curriculum in place nor were there any textbooks. She walked into the classroom with weeks of experience to date. Children were running everywhere. There was a child that regularly liked to sit on top of the lockers. There were no rules, no routine and zero culture. Those students were just mad at the world. After she'd been there for about ten days, a child asked if Jami was going to leave them too. Jami said she wasn't going anywhere and made sure she was there every day.   Coming from an environment where you could go to anyone and they would help you to an environment where she was, literally, working in isolation, Jami learned the importance of building relationships with students, having the support of colleagues and working with them. By the end of that year, she had gotten the students to the point where they actually believed that their teacher really did care for them, love them, and would work for them. Every year since she taught that class, even when she moves to a new place, she tries to make sure that she builds the culture in her classroom first.

Scan for the full episode.

Jami stayed in education when a lot of people would have left. She was the fifth teacher for that group of students, but she built those relationships and ended up making it. Even though her journey started out as a struggle, Jami took it as a learning experience. If she hadn't gone through that trench, she would never have learned so much about the importance of building relationships with the students she taught. She also knows how important it is, now as a principal, to reach out to new teachers and check in with them regularly.

Some of the trench stories in this book may shed a bit of a negative light on educational experiences, but these stories don't frame every educator's experience. Think of what you have learned and grown from due to your experiences. Focus on the positive times and positive experiences you have gained.

While you may think what happens to you is out of your control, much of what happens is about how you handle or react to the situation. On my phone's home screen, I keep the inspirational words: Life is 10% what happens to you and 90% how you react to it. Things that often happen by fate, such as losing a job by position elimination, being hired in a new district, being diagnosed with a disease, or being cured, are usually out of your hands. Yet, you can't grumble about the fact that you're stuck in the situation unless you decide to do something about it.

Consider these questions:
- Wouldn't you want to learn more to improve your skills if you were forced to look for a new position?
- If you've been diagnosed with a disease, wouldn't you want to do as much research as you can on the best treatment options out there?
- When you must get treatment for the disease, wouldn't you want to go into that treatment with the most positive mindset you can?
- Don't you want to be proactive to whatever challenge comes rather than being reactive?

Conclusion

As this book concludes, I would like to add that all of us have had to try many times before we've encountered success or felt like we've made our way out of the trenches. Here is a list of some things I had to try many times before I finally succeeded:

- Passing Algebra II in high school – I had to take one semester of the class twice. Finally, on the third try, my last semester of high school, I scraped by with a D. I needed it to graduate!

- Being told, after graduating high school, and securing a spot at a *gymnas* (high school-13th grade) in Norway, that I had to go back to the U.S. because I couldn't obtain a student visa when there as an independent high school student (only as a college or exchange high school student). After about six weeks of working with a lawyer, I had to head back to the States in October of that school year. I took my books with me (this was before online coursework) and even took one semester of freshman college requirements at Tulsa University. Then, I took the necessary exams in May the following year and gained the high school equivalency to enter the University of Tromsø, which I attended and completed my BA.

- During my first semester of university, not passing "ex. Phil." (a mandatory philosophy course) – I took the course and retook the exam twice that first semester. After not passing those three times, I put off ex. Phil until the last semester of my BA studies some five years later. *I finally passed on my fourth try*!
- Having my position teaching French eliminated *three years in a row* in the late 2000s due to projected low enrollment at the school, other languages coming in and eliminations of World Language teachers. When I couldn't get another teaching job in 2009, I started the principal licensure program and completed the internship while pregnant with and after delivering my daughter. I also added an English Language Arts endorsement to my teaching license.
- I had to take one of the Program for Licensing Assessments for Colorado Educators (PLACE) exams for Colorado certification *eight times before I finally passed*, over a period of three and a half years.
- Having countless interviews for but not landing a job in school leadership for *seven years* – I finished the program in 2011, finally broke into school leadership in 2018.

Take a moment and write a list of things YOU may have struggled with but persisted in, then finally broke through. You may want to go back to your high school years (or earlier), as I did. You may want to keep it professional and only mention failures and resiliency stories in your career, or add some personal challenges you have experienced along the way as well.

Sometimes, I would get caught up in negative thought loops for a long time and wonder how to stop the cycle of frustration. Finally, I realized that *I can only do what I have been doing*- which is to keep moving forward. The term "trenches" doesn't need to have a negative connotation. Trenches are what you make them and how you view them in your work.

I would like to wrap up my thoughts by referring to Sir Elton John's song, *I'm Still Standing*. While I have been through many trenches along the way during my educational career, I have persevered. I have learned and grown from different experiences. I have not given up on my pursuit of achieving the next level. I am a testimony to those who are faced with day-to-day challenges in education. Even after all these years, "I'm still standing, better than I ever did." I choose to stay, will you?

Recommendations to Improve Your Practice

What do you do to reflect on your practice? Professionally, I seek to constantly improve my practice through reading books by other educators and attending conferences and other professional development.

Scan for the full book list.

A list of books that I recommend are:
- *Engagement is Not a Unicorn, (It's a Narwhal): Mind-Changing Theory and Strategies That Will Create Real Engagement (workbook follow-up)* by Heather Lyon
- *10 Mindframes for Visible Learning: Teaching for Success* by John Hattie and Klaus Zierer, et al.
- *Becoming the Educator They Need: Strategies, Mindsets, and Beliefs for Supporting Male Black and Latino Students* by Robert Jackson
- *Creating a Culture of Reflective Practice: Building Capacity for Schoolwide Success* by Pete Hall & Alisa Simera
- *The Burnout Cure: Learning to Love Teaching Again* by Chase Mielke
- *Cultural Competence Now: 56 Exercises to Help Educators Understand and Challenge Bias, Racism, and Privilege* by Vernita Mayfield

- Books School Leaders Should Read-Better Leaders Better Schools List by Danny Bauer of Better Leaders, Better Schools

Personally, I have been an avid listener of three podcasts for school leaders for over four years. These include:
- Better leaders, Better Schools
- Principal Center Radio
- Transformative Principal

I recommend these podcasts on school culture and teacher motivation:
- School Culture by Design
- The Burned-In Teacher

Twitter is a HUGE source of PD for educators. Whether it's by reading articles or listening to podcasts that are shared, watching Tic Tok videos by other educators, or viewing live broadcasts, there is so much to learn. Here is a list of my recommended educators to follow on Twitter:

- ZARETTA HAMMOND- @Ready4rigor –Author and Literacy Advocate
- JESSICA JOHNSON- @PrincipalJ- Awuthor of *The Coach Approach* & *Balance Like a Pirate*
- SARAH JOHNSON- @SarahSajohnson- Co-Author of *Balance like a Pirate* & *Lead with Faith*

- BARUTI KAFELE- @Principalkafele- Author of *The Assistant Principal 50, The Aspiring Principal 50, The Principal 50 & Is My School a Better School because I lead it?*

- IBRAM X. KENDI- @DrIbram – Author of *How to be an Anti-Racist*

- JONATHAN ALSHEIMER- @mr_Alsheimer – Author of *Next Level Teaching*

- JIMMY CASAS- @casas_jimmy – Author of *Culturize & Live your Excellence*

- DANNY STEELE- @SteeleThoughts – Author of *Essential Truths for Teachers & Essential Truths for Principals*

- LAURA ROBB- @LRobbTeacher – Author of *The Reading Intervention Toolkit* and *Read Talk Write*

- EVAN ROBB- @ERobbPrincipal - Principal, TEDx Speaker, Author of *The 10-Minute Principal*

Tweet me at @danagoodier if you have a trench story to share and would be interested in being a guest on the podcast!

Acknowledgements

I would like to thank my publisher, Road to Awesome- Darrin and Jessica Peppard for their support during the writing and editing of this manuscript. I would also like to thank other Road to Awesome authors for their support, tips and dialogue about being first time writers. Finally, I want to acknowledge the many colleagues who provided praise pieces for this book. Your reading of the manuscript and positive feedback is greatly appreciated!

References

Baruti Kafele. (2021, October 2). *Closing the "attitude gap" in your classrooms - virtual AP leadership academy (Week 75).* YouTube. Retrieved February 23, 2022, from https://www.youtube.com/watch?v=G_Tu9e1i1s8

Beck, B. (2020). *Unlocking Unlimited Potential.* Codebreaker

Breyer, R. (2021). *Taking the Leap: A Field Guide For Aspiring School Leaders.* Road to Awesome, LLC.

Brown, B. (2020, August 10). Insider. mindspocom. Retrieved December 2, 2022, from https://mindspo.com/2020/08/10/brene-browns-top-10-rules-for-self-love/

Buck, F. (2021). *Get Organized, Digitally!: The Educator's Guide to Time Management.* Taylor & Francis

Cabeen, J. (2019). *Lead with Grace: Leaning into the soft skills of leadership.* Times 10 Publications.

Garcia, H. and Miralles, F. (2017) *Ikigai: The Japanese Secret to a Long and Healthy Life.* Penguin Books

Goodier, D. (2021, November 13). *Practicing gratitude daily.* Teach Better. Retrieved February 22, 2022, from https://www.teachbetter.com/blog/practicing-gratitude-on-a-daily-basis/

Goodier, D. (2021, October 17). *Finding your PD niche*. Teach Better. Retrieved February 22, 2022, from https://www.teachbetter.com/blog/finding-your-pd-niche/

Goodier, D. (2021, September 10). *Improving stakeholder communication*. Teach Better. Retrieved February 22, 2022, from https://www.teachbetter.com/blog/improving-stakeholder-communication/

Goodier, D. (2021, March 4). *Be a leader who empowers your staff*. Teach Better. Retrieved February 22, 2022, from https://www.teachbetter.com/blog/be-a-leader-who-empowers-your-staff/

Goodier, D. (2020, June 3). Episode #3: Mechele Newell. Out of the Trenches podcast [audio podcast episode]. https://youtu.be/3Y4tfNMY_6I

Goodier, D. (2020, August 19). episode #14: Jessica Johnson. Out of the Trenches podcast [audio podcast episode]. https://youtu.be/F6Z6zq4FbmY

Goodier, D. (2020, August 26). episode #15: Amber Harper. Out of the Trenches podcast [audio podcast episode]. https://youtu.be/C4K3p2KdfbA

Goodier, D. (2020, October 14). episode #23: Rick Jetter. Out of the Trenches podcast [audio podcast episode]. https://youtu.be/ssl_gFHxfPA

Goodier, D. (2020, November 4). Episode #26: Sarah Thomas. Out of the Trenches podcast [audio podcast episode]. https://danagoodier.com/my-podcast-show-notes-4/

Goodier, D. (2020, November 11). episode #27: Danny Brassell. Out of the Trenches podcast [audio podcast episode]. Danny Brassell https://youtu.be/44fqZaay71Q

Goodier, D. (2021, March 31). Episode #34: Steven Gupton. Out of the Trenches podcast [audio podcast episode]. https://www.youtube.com/watch?v=r7GCCPhCTuI

Goodier, D. (2021, January 10). episode #41: Sherianna Boyle. Out of the Trenches podcast [audio podcast episode]. https://youtu.be/lZgtYk_QpcA

Goodier, D. (2021, January 13). episode #42: Danny Bauer. Out of the Trenches podcast [audio podcast episode]. https://danagoodier.com/my-podcast-show-notes-6/

Goodier, D. (2021, February 9). episode #54: Matt Miller. Out of the Trenches podcast [audio podcast episode]. Matt Miller https://youtu.be/MD2tefShKl4

Goodier, D. (2021, March 14). episode #59: Jim Sporleder. Out of the Trenches podcast [audio podcast episode]. Jim Sporleder https://youtu.be/YIO4SnIUPfs

Goodier, D. (2021, July 15). episode #93: Jami Fowler-White. Out of the Trenches podcast [audio podcast episode]. https://danagoodier.com/podcast-show-notes-3/

Goodier, D. (2021, July 18). Episode #94: Tyson Gardin. Out of the Trenches podcast [audio podcast episode]. https://danagoodier.com/podcast-show-notes-3/

Goodier, D. (2021, October 3). episode #114: Orly Wahba. Out of the Trenches podcast [audio podcast episode]. https://youtu.be/HHlY6vl-A0U

Goodier, D. (2021, October 13). episode #116: Frank Buck. Out of the Trenches podcast [audio podcast episode]. https://open.spotify.com/episode/https://danagoodier.com/episodes-115-123/

Hlabangana-Clay, Ann. (2021, April, 20). episode #30: Dana Goodier. Coaching You Through All Things Education [audio podcast episode]. https://anchor.fm/coachingallthingsedu/episodes/Episode-30-A-Conversation-with-Dr--Dana-Goodier-about-the-Future-of-Education-and-the-Part-We-Play-eu862t/a-a49aieg

John, Elton. "I'm Still Standing." Too Low For Zero. EMI Records. 1983. Vinyl.

Molitor, J. (2019). *The happy teacher's handbook: From overwhelmed to inspired: Helping teachers embrace resiliency*. Lift up Leaders, LLC.

About the Author

Dr. Dana Goodier has worked in education since 1999. She has taught World Languages, multilingual learners and English Language Arts. She has served as a middle school administrator, elementary school behavior interventionist, high school gifted and talented coordinator, and World Language Department Chair. She serves on the board of directors for the Colorado Congress of Foreign Language Teachers (CCFLT) and Denver Women's Chorus (DWC).

Dana completed her doctorate in Educational Leadership in early 2020. For her dissertation, she researched reasons parents were opting their students out of high-stakes testing at middle schools between 2014-2019 and how that affected the district accreditation rating. She wrote professional development (PD) modules for staff and parents as part of her capstone project. Dana writes blogs on a bi-monthly basis for Teach Better Team. Many of these blogs are her observations of day-to-day happenings in the life of educators.

Dana often speaks at conferences, providing educators with techniques to minimize off-task behavior and increase time on task, find your PD niche and several other topics. She is the host of the *Out of the Trenches* podcast, which features educators who share their stories of resiliency. Follow her on Twitter and LinkedIn @danagoodier and on Instagram @outoftrenchespc

Work With Dana

Dana is available for in-person or virtual professional development training at your school or district. Please visit her website www.danagoodier.com to see the many topics on which she can help your staff including: classroom management and student engagement, evaluation of needs based on your school improvement plan, work with PLCs in finding their PD niche, getting into classrooms often as an instructional leader and discipline/attendance support. Dana has spoken professionally since 2017 and working with staff is her passion! You can book a consultation with her at: www.calendly.com/dagoo/15m.

More Books From Road to Awesome

Taking the Leap: A Field Guide for Aspiring School Leaders by Robert F. Breyer

Transform: Techy Notes to Make Learning Sticky by Debbie Tannenbaum

Becoming Principal: A Leadership Journey & The Story of School Community by Dr. Jeff Prickett

Elevate Your Vibe: Action Planning with Purpose by Lisa Toebben

#OwnYourEpic: Leadership Lessons in Owning Your Voice and Your Story by Dr. Jay Dostal

The Design Thinking, Entrepreneurial, Visionary Planning Leader: A Practical guide for Thriving in Ambiguity by Dr. Michael Nagler

Becoming the Change: Five Essential Elements to Being Your Best Self by Dan Wolfe

inspired: moments that matter by Melissa Wright

Foundations of Instructional Coaching: Impact People, Improve Instruction, Increase Success by Ashley Hubner

Out of the Trenches: Stories of Resilient Educators by Dana Goodier
Principled Leader

by Bobby Pollicino

Road to Awesome: The Journey of a Leader
by Darrin Peppard

When Calling Parents Isn't Your Calling: A teacher's guide to communicating with all parents
by Crystal Frommert

Struggle to Strength: Finding the Ingredients to Your Secret Sauce
by Kip Shubert

Guiding Transformational Change in Education
by Kristina V. Mattis

Kids Books From Road to Awesome

Road to Awesome A Journey for Kids
by Jillian DuBois and Darrin M. Peppard

Emersyn Blake and the Spotted Salamander
by Kim Collazo

Theodore Edward Makes a New Friend
by Alyssa Schmidt

I'm Autistic and I'm Awesome
by Derek Danziger

Emersyn Blake and the Stalked Jellyfish
by Kim Collazo

https://roadtoawesome.net/books

www.ingramcontent.com/pod-product-compliance
Lightning Source LLC
Chambersburg PA
CBHW072010090426
42734CB00033B/2414